Clarence Winthrop Bowen

Woodstock

An historical Sketch

Clarence Winthrop Bowen

Woodstock
An historical Sketch

ISBN/EAN: 9783337116385

Printed in Europe, USA, Canada, Australia, Japan

Cover: Foto ©ninafisch / pixelio.de

More available books at **www.hansebooks.com**

WOODSTOCK

AN HISTORICAL SKETCH

BY

CLARENCE WINTHROP BOWEN, Ph.D.

READ AT ROSELAND PARK, WOODSTOCK, CONNECTICUT, AT THE BI-CENTENNIAL CELEBRATION
OF THE TOWN, ON TUESDAY, SEPTEMBER 7, 1886

———

NEW YORK & LONDON
G. P. PUTNAM'S SONS
The Knickerbocker Press
1886

Press of
G. P. Putnam's Sons
New York

As a full history of Woodstock has been in preparation for several years and will, it is hoped, be published in the course of another year, this brief sketch is issued as it was read at the Bi-Centennial Anniversary of the town.

CONTENTS.

I.

The history of the town of Woodstock is associated with the beginnings of history in New England. The ideas of the first settlers of Woodstock were the ideas of the first settlers of the Colony of Plymouth and the Province of Massachusetts Bay. The planting of these colonies was one of the fruits of the Reformation. The antagonism between the Established Church of England and the Non-Conformists led to the settlement of New England. The Puritans of Massachusetts, at first Non-Conformists, became Separatists like the Pilgrims of Plymouth. Pilgrims and Puritans alike accepted persecution and surrendered the comforts of home to obtain religious liberty. They found it in New England ; and here, more quickly than in the mother country, they developed also that civil liberty which is now the birthright of every Anglo-Saxon.

II.

The settlement of Woodstock is intimately connected
with the first organized settlement on Massachusetts
Bay ; and how our mother town of Roxbury was first
established is best told in the words of Thomas Dudley
in his letter to the Countess of Lincoln under date of
Boston, March 12, 1630–1 :

" About the year 1627 some friends, being together
in Lincolnshire, fell into discourse about New England
and the planting of the gospel there. In 1628 we
procured a patent from his Majesty for our planting
between the Massachusetts Bay and Charles River
on the South and the River of Merrimack on the
North and three miles on either side of those rivers
and bay .   .   .   and the same year we sent Mr. John
Endicott and some with him to begin a plantation. In
1629 we sent divers ships over with about three hundred
people. Mr. Winthrop, of Suffolk (who was well
known in his own country and well approved here for
his piety, liberality, wisdom, and gravity), coming in to
us we came to such resolution that in April, 1630, we
set sail from Old England. . . . We were forced to
change counsel, and, for our present shelter, to plant
dispersedly."

Settlements were accordingly made at Salem, Charlestown, Boston, Medford, Watertown, and in several other localities. The sixth settlement was made, to quote further from the same letter to the Countess of Lincoln, by " others of us two miles from Boston, in a place we named Rocksbury." [1]

The date of settlement was September 28, 1630, and just three weeks later the first General Court that ever sat in America was held in Boston. The same year the first church in Boston was organized.[2] Roxbury, like the other settlements of Massachusetts Bay, was a little republic in itself. The people chose the selectmen and governed themselves; and as early as 1634, like the seven other organized towns, they sent three deputies to Boston to attend the first representative Assembly at which important business was transacted. The government of Roxbury, like the other plantations, was founded on a theocratic basis. Church and state were inseparable. No one could be admitted as a citizen unless he was a member of the church. Many of the first settlers came from Nazing, a small village in England, about twenty miles from London, on the river Lee. Morris, Ruggles, Payson, and Peacock, names read in the earliest records of Woodstock, were old family names in Nazing. Other first inhabitants of Roxbury came from Wales and the west of England, or London and its vicinity. Among the

---

[1] Also spelt Roxberry, Roxborough, Rocksborough.   [2] July 30, 1630.

founders were John Johnson, Richard Bugbee, and John Leavens, whose family names are well known as among the first settlers of Woodstock. All were men of property[1]; none were "of the poorer sort." In 1631 the Rev. John Eliot, a native of the village of Nazing, arrived with a company of Nazing pilgrims. Eliot, though earnestly solicited to become pastor of the church in Boston,[2] accepted the charge of the church in Roxbury, which was organized in 1632,[3] and was the sixth church, in order of time, established in New England. Another name equally prominent in the earliest years of the history of Roxbury was that of William Pynchon, afterwards known as the founder of Springfield in Massachusetts. Only Boston excels Roxbury in the number of its citizens who have made illustrious the early history of the Massachusetts colony.[4] Among the early settlers of Roxbury who themselves became, or whose descendants became, the early settlers of Woodstock, were the Bartholomews, Bowens, Bugbees, Chandlers, Childs, Corbins, Crafts, Griggses, Gareys, Holmeses, Johnsons, Lyons, Levinses, Mays, Morrises, Paysons, Peacocks, Peakes, Perrins, Scarboroughs, and Williamses.[5]

[1] Young's "Chronicles of Massachusetts," p. 396.
[2] Winthrop's "Journal," by Savage, vol. i., p. 111.
[3] "Ordained over the First Church, Nov. 5, 1632."—Eliot's tomb in Roxbury.
[4] "Memorial History of Boston," vol. i., p. 403.
[5] Though the Williamses did not settle permanently in Woodstock till some years after the first settlement, the family was most prominent in Roxbury, and one of its representatives visited the grant officially in 1686.

In 1643 the towns within the jurisdiction of Massachusetts had grown to thirty, and Roxbury did more than
her share towards the organization of the new towns.
In fact, Roxbury has been called the mother of towns,
no less than fifteen communities having been founded
by her citizens.[1]   Among the most important of these
settlements was the town of Woodstock, whose Bi-
centennial we this day celebrate.

[1] Drake's " Town of Roxbury " and " Memorial History of Boston," vol. i.,
pp. 401–422.

III.

A glance at the country about us previous to the settlement of the town, in 1686, shows us a land sparsely inhabited by small bands of peaceful Indians, without an independent chief of their own, but who paid tribute to the Sachem of the Mohegans, the warriors who had revolted from the Pequots. Woodstock was a portion of the Nipmuck[1] country, so-called because it contained fresh ponds or lakes in contrast to other sections that bordered upon the sea or along running rivers. Wabbaquasset, or the mat-producing place, was the name of the principal Indian village, and that name still exists in the corrupted form of Quasset to designate a section of the town. Indians from the Nipmuck[2] country took corn to Boston in 1630, soon after the arrival of the "Bay Colony"; and in 1633[3] John Oldman and his three Dorchester companions passed through this same section on their way to learn something of the Connecticut River country; and they

---

[1] De Forest's "Indians of Connecticut," and Palfrey's "History of New England," and Miss Ellen D. Larned's "History of Windham County."

[2] Also "called the Wabbaquassett and Whetstone country; and sometimes the Mohegan conquered country, as Uncas had conquered and added it to his sachemdom." Trumbull's "History of Connecticut," vol. i., 31.

[3] September.

may have rested on yonder "Plaine Hill," for history states that they "lodged at Indians towns all the way." [1] The old " Connecticut Path" over which that distinguished band [2] of colonists went in 1635 and 1636 to settle the towns of Windsor, Wethersfield, and Hartford, passed through the heart of what is now Woodstock. [3] This path so famous in the early days of New England history, came out of Thompson Woods, a little north of Woodstock Lake, and proceeding across the Senexet meadow, ran west near Plaine Hill, Marcy's Hill, and a little south of the base of Coatney Hill. For more than fifty years before the settlement of the town, this historic path near Woodstock Hill was the outlet for the surplus population of Massachusetts Bay

[1] Winthrop's " Journal," by Savage, vol. i.. 132. Palfrey's " Hist. of New England," vol. i., 369. The same year (Nov. 1633), "Samuel Hall and two other persons travelled westward into the country as far as this [Connecticut] river." Holmes' " Annals," vol. i., 220.

[2] Winthrop's " Journal," vol. i., 171.

[3] Possibly some of the Dorchester emigrants, including Henry Wolcott, William Phelps, and others, may have passed a little south of this line. Dr. McClure's MSS., in the possession of the Connecticut Historical Society : " In a conversation with the late aged and respectable Capt. Sabin of Pomfret, Ct., he related to me the following discovery, viz. : About forty years ago he felled a large and ancient yoke about the north line of Pomfret adjoining Woodstock. On cutting within some inches of the heart of the tree it was seen to have been cut and chipped with some short tool like an axe. Rightly judging that at the time when it must have been done the Indians so far inland were destitute and ignorant of the use of iron tools, he counted the number of the annual circular rings from the said marks to the bark of the tree, and found that there were as many rings as the years which had intervened from the migration of the Dorchester party to that time. Hence ' the probability that they had journeyed along the north border of Pomfret, and as they traveled by a compass, the conjecture is corroborated by that course being nearly in a direct line from Boston to the place of their settlement on the Connecticut River.' "—Stiles' " History of Ancient Windsor," p. 26.

and the line of communication between Massachusetts and the Connecticut and New Haven colonies. But the most noteworthy feature in the description of the Indians of the Nipmuck country is that as early as 1670 they were formed into Praying Villages. Evidently the instructions of Gov. Cradock in his letter of March, 1629, to John Endicott had not been forgotten. In that letter he said : " Be not unmindful of the main end of our plantation by endeavoring to bring the Indians to the knowledge of the gospel." In the heart of one man at least that idea was paramount. John Eliot, the Apostle to the Indians, was not content to be simply the pastor of the church of Roxbury for nearly sixty years. Amid his countless other labors he preached the gospel to the Indians of the Nipmuck country. The first Indian church in America had been established by him at Natick in 1651 ; and, in 1674, he visited the Indian villages in the wild territory about these very hills. As he found it, to quote his own words,[1] " absolutely necessary to carry on civility with religion," he was accompanied by Major Daniel Gookin, who had been appointed, in 1656, magistrate of all the Indian towns. Maanexit was first visited on the Mohegan or Quinebaug River, near what is now New Boston, where Eliot preached to the natives, using as his text the seventh verse of the twenty-fourth Psalm : " Lift up your heads, O ye gates ; and

[1] "Memorial Hist. of Boston," vol. i., 263.

be ye lift up, ye everlasting doors ; and the king of glory shall come in."

Quinnatisset, on what is now Thompson Hill, was the name of another Praying Town. But a quotation[1] from the homely narrative of Major Gookin is the best description of Eliot's memorable visit to Woodstock :

" We went not to it [Quinnatisset], being straitened for time, but we spake with some of the principal people at Wabquissit.[2] . . . Wabquissit . . . lieth about nine or ten miles from Maanexit, upon the west side, six miles of Mohegan River, and is distant from Boston west and by south, about seventy-two miles. It lieth about four miles within the Massachusetts south line. It hath about thirty families, and one hundred and fifty souls. It is situated in a very rich soil, manifested by the goodly crop of Indian corn then newly ingathered, not less than forty bushels upon an acre. We came thither late in the evening upon the 15th of September, and took up our quarters at the sagamore's wigwam, who was not at home : but his squaw courteously admitted us, and provided liberally, in their way, for the Indians that accompanied us. This sagamore inclines to religion, and keeps the meeting on sabbath days at his house, which is spacious, about sixty feet in length and twenty feet in width. The teacher of this place is named Sampson ; an active and ingenious person. He speaks good

[1] "Historical Collections of the Indians in New England. By Daniel Gookin, Gentleman, Printed from the original manuscript, 1792." See " Collections Mass. Hist. Soc.," vol. i., First Series, pp. 190–192.
[2] Wabbaquasset, or Woodstock.

English and reads well. He is brother unto Joseph,
before named, teacher at Chabanakougkomun¹ . . .
being both hopeful, pious, and active men ; especially
the younger before-named Sampson, teacher at Wabquissit, who was, a few years since, a dissolute person,
and I have been forced to be severe in punishing him
for his misdemeanors formerly. But now he is,
through grace, changed and become sober and pious ;
and he is now very thankful to me for the discipline
formerly exercised towards him. And besides his
flagitious life heretofore, he lived very uncomfortably
with his wife ; but now they live very well together,
I confess this story is a digression. But because it
tendeth to magnify grace, and that to a prodigal, and
to declare how God remembers his covenant unto the
children of such as are faithful and zealous for him in
their time and generation, I have mentioned it.

" We being at Wabquissit, at the sagamore's wigwam, divers of the principal people that were at home
came to us, with whom we spent a good part of the
night in prayer, singing psalms, and exhortations.
There was a person among them, who, sitting mute a
great space, at last spake to this effect : That he was
agent for Unkas, Sachem of Mohegan, who challenged
right to, and dominion over, this people of Wabquissit.
And said he, Unkas is not well pleased that the English should pass over Mohegan River to call his Indians
to pray to God. Upon which speech Mr. Eliot first
answered, that it was his work to call upon all men
everywhere, as he had opportunity, especially the
Indians, to repent and embrace the gospel ; but he did

¹ Dudley.

not meddle with civil right or jurisdiction. When he had done speaking, then I declared to him, and desired him to inform Unkas what I said, that Wabquissit was within the jurisdiction of Massachusetts, and that the government of that people did belong to them ; and that they do look upon themselves concerned to promote the good of all people within their limits, especially if they embraced Christianity. Yet it was not hereby intended to abridge the Indian sachems of their just and ancient right over the Indians, in respect of paying tribute or any other dues. But the main design of the English was to bring them to the good knowledge of God in Christ Jesus; and to suppress among them those sins of drunkenness, idolatry, powowing or witchcraft, whoredom, murder, and like sins. As for the English, they had taken no tribute from them, nor taxed them with any thing of the kind.

"Upon the 16th day of September[1] being at Wabquissit, as soon as the people were come together, Mr. Eliot first prayed, and then preached to them, in their own language, out of Mat. vi., 33 : *First seek the kingdom of heaven and the righteousness thereof, and all these things shall be added unto you.* Their teacher, Sampson, first reading and setting the cxix. Ps., 1st part, which was sung. The exercise was concluded with prayer.

"Then I began a Court among the Indians, and first I approved their teacher, Sampson, and their constable, Black James,[2] giving each of them a charge to be dili-

[1] 1674.

[2] Black James was a distinguished Indian. He met Eliot again in Cambridge in June of 1681, where a meeting of the claimants of the Nipmuck country was held. The village and much of the land of the town of Dudley was known years after the settlement of Woodstock as "The Land of Black James and Company."—Ammidown's "Historical Collections," vol. i., 406, 461.

gent and faithful in their places. Also I exhorted the
people to yield obedience to the gospel of Christ and
to those set in order there. Then published a warrant
or order, that I had prepared, empowering the constable to suppress drunkenness, Sabbath breaking,
especially powowing and idolatry. And, after warning
given, to apprehend all delinquents and bring them
before authority to answer for their misdoings ; the
smaller faults to bring before Watasacompamun, ruler
of the Nipmuck country ; for idolatry and powowing
to bring them before me : So we took leave of this
people of Wabquissit, and about eleven o'clock returned back to Maanexit and Chabanakougkomun,
where we lodged this night."

History fails to locate the spot where John Eliot's
sermon to the Indians of Woodstock was delivered,
but tradition points to " Pulpit Rock," so-called, under
the aged chestnut trees of the McClellan farm near
the " Old Hall " [1] road.

But Eliot's good work in the Nipmuck country was
destroyed when King Philip's war broke out in 1675.
In August of that year a company of Providence men
journeyed as far as Wabbaquasset, thinking that
possibly King Philip himself had escaped thither.[2]
They found an Indian fort a mile or two west of
Woodstock Hill, but no Indians. A party from Nor-
wich in June of the following year also found deserted
Wabbaquasset and the other Praying Villages. Deso-

[1] Named after " Wabbaquasset Hall," built in the spring or summer of 1686.
[2] Palfrey's " History of New England," vol. iii., 159.

lation and devastation followed the disappearance of
the Red Man. The Nipmuck country became more a
wilderness than ever, forsaken of its aboriginal inhabitants whose barbaric tenure could not stand against a
superior civilization.

> " Forgotten race, farewell ! Your haunts we tread,
> Our mighty rivers speak your words of yore,
> Our mountains wear them on their misty head,
> Our sounding cataracts hurl them to the shore ;
> But on the lake your flashing oar is still,
> Hush'd is your hunter's cry on dale and hill,
> Your arrow stays the eagle's flight no more,
> And ye, like troubled shadows, sink to rest
> In unremember'd tombs, unpitied and unbless'd." [1]

[1] Mrs. L. H. Sigourney's " Pocahontas."

IV.

The time had now arrived for the white man to make a settlement at Wabbaquasset. In May, of 1681, the General Court of Massachusetts Bay had given to William Stoughton and Joseph Dudley the care of the Nipmuck country, with power to ascertain the titles belonging to the Indians and others, and a meeting of the claimants was held the following month at Cambridge, at which John Eliot rendered much assistance as interpreter. Dudley and Stoughton purchased all the claims, and the following year,[1] the whole Nipmuck country became the property of Massachusetts Bay. Jurisdiction over the country had already been claimed, under the terms of the Massachusetts charter. Many of the inhabitants of the town of Roxbury now felt that they could improve their condition and increase their usefulness by forming a settlement in some desirable portion of the new country. Undoubtedly their pastor, John Eliot, had told them of the beauty and fertility of the country about the Praying Villages of Maanexit, Quinnatisset, and

---

[1] Feb. 10, 1682.

20

Wabbaquasset.[1] Town meetings to arrange for a new settlement, were held in Roxbury in October of 1683.[2] A petition was signed, by a number of representative citizens of the town, asking that the General Court might grant to them a tract seven miles square about Quinnatisset, in the Nipmuck country. All save six of the thirty-six who signed this petition, afterwards became settlers of the new town, and of the five selectmen of Roxbury who presented the petition to the General Court, three[3] represented families prominent in the early history of Woodstock. The General Court at once granted[4] the petition provided the grant should not fall within a section to be reserved for Messrs Stoughton and Dudley, and Major Thompson, and provided also that thirty families should be settled on the plantation within three years from the following June, "and mainteyne amongst them an able, orthodox, godly minister."[5] In 1684 Roxbury accepted the terms of the General Court, and sent Samuel and John Ruggles, John Curtis, and Edward Morris, as a committe of four, to "view the wilderness and find a convenient place."

[1] Ellis' "History of Roxbury Town": "When the people of Roxbury came to take up lands, they selected their locations amongst the praying Indians or where Indians had been converted to Christianity. . . . This certainly is a sure indication of the steady adherence of his [John Eliot's] fellow-townsmen and their belief in the actual benefits of his missionary labors."

[2] Oct. 6, 10, and 17.

[3] Joseph Griggs, John Ruggles, and Edward Morris.

[4] Dec. 5, 1683.

[5] "Records of the Governor and Company of Massachusetts Bay in New England," vol. v., 426.

As Quinnatisset had been in part already granted, the committee reported[1] a territory " commodiose " for settlement at " Seneksuk and Wapagusset and the lands ajasiant." A committee was therefore appointed to draw up an agreement for the "goers," as they were called, to sign. In 1685,[2] in answer to the petition of Edward Morris, deputy in behalf of the town of Roxbury, the General Court extended the limit of the time of settlement from June 10, 1687, to Jan. 31, 1688, and granted freedom from rates up to that time.[3] At town meetings held in Roxbury, during the same year, it was arranged that one half of the grant should belong to the new settlers and one hundred pounds in money be given to them in instalments of twenty pounds a year, and the other half of the grant should belong to " the stayers " in consideration of the aid given " the goers." The southern half of the grant was the portion subsequently occupied by " the goers." Actual possession, however, was not taken until April of the following year. On the second page of the cover of the old and musty first volume of records of the proprietors of New Roxbury, afterwards called Woodstock, are these words :

" April 5, 1686.

" These are the thirteen who were sent out to spy out Woodstock as planters and to take actual poses-

---

[1] Oct. 27, 1684.   [2] Jan. 28th.

[3] " Records of the Governor and Company of the Massachusetts Bay in New England," vol. v., 468.

sion : Jonathan Smithers, John Frissell, Nathaniel Garey, John Marcy, Benjamin Griggs, John Lord, Benjamin Sabin, Henry Bowen, Matthew Davis, Thomas Bacon, Peter Aspinwall, George Griggs, and Ebenezer Morris."

These thirteen planters, or the " Old Thirteen " as they have always been called, were visited in May or June [1] by a committee who had been appointed to ascertain the bounds of the grant. The last meeting of the "goers to settle" was held in Roxbury, July 21st ; their first meeting in New Roxbury was held August 25th. A committee of seven, consisting of Joseph Griggs, Edward Morris, Henry Bowen, Sr., John Chandler, Sr., Samuel Craft, Samuel Scarborough, and Jonathan Smithers, having been appointed to make needful arrangements preliminary to the drawing of home lots, that drawing took place on the twenty-eighth of August, or, by the new style of reckoning time, exactly two hundred years ago to-day.

Say the old records : " After solemn prayer to God, who is the Disposer of all things, they drew lots according to the agreement, every man being satisfied and contented with God's disposing." Would that the words of that prayer and the picture of that scene could to-day be reproduced ! Surely the spirit of the Puritans of 1630 was the spirit of that band of pilgrims in 1686 on yonder hill. These are the honored names

[1] Committee appointed May 14, 1686, and reported to Roxbury June 12th.

of the first settlers : Thomas and Joseph Bacon, James
Corbin, Benjamin Sabin, Henry Bowen, Thomas
Lyon, Ebenezer Morris, Matthew Davis, William
Lyon, Sr., John Chandler, Sr., Peter Aspinwall,
John Frizzel, Joseph Frizzel, Jonathan Smithers, John
Butcher, Jonathan Davis, Jonathan Peake, Nathaniel
Garey, John Bowen, Nathaniel Johnson, John Hub-
bard, George Griggs, Benjamin Griggs, William Lyon,
Jr., John Leavens, Nathaniel Sanger, Samuel Scar-
borough, Samuel Craft, Samuel May, Joseph Bugbee,
Samuel Peacock, Arthur Humphrey, John Bugbee,
Jr., Andrew Watkins, John Marcy, Edward Morris,
Joseph Peake, John Holmes, and John Chandler, Jr.

Of that list of thirty-nine,[1] Benjamin Sabin, Nathaniel
Sanger, Nathaniel Garey, John Hubbard, Matthew
Davis, and George Griggs afterwards moved to Pom-
fret; Peter Aspinwall and his step-sons, the sons of
John Leavens, went to Killingby; and Arthur Hum-
phrey and others became the first settlers of Ashford.
A few returned to Roxbury. But a large share of
the original settlers lived and died in Woodstock,
including Edward and Ebenezer Morris, Jonathan
and Joseph Peake, James Corbin, Thomas and
Joseph Bacon, Henry Bowen, William and Thomas
Lyon, John Chandler, Sr., and John Chandler, Jr.,
John Butcher, Nathaniel Johnson, Joseph and John

[1] Though the name of John Ruggles was on the list of "goers" and a house
lot was drawn for him, he did not settle in Woodstock. The family of Ruggles is prominent among the first settlers in Pomfret.

Bugbee, John Marcy, John Holmes, and perhaps a few others. As an illustration of the ages of the pioneers in 1686, it may be mentioned that Benjamin Griggs was nineteen; Joseph Bacon and Andrew Watkins, twenty; John Bugbee, John Chandler, Jr., James Corbin, and Jonathan Davis, twenty-one; Peter Aspinwall, Matthew Davis, John Frizzel, and Lieut. Ebenezer Morris, twenty-two; John Butcher and Nathaniel Garcy, twenty-three; John Bowen and John Marcy, twenty-four; George Griggs, John Holmes, and Samuel May, twenty-five; Thomas Bacon, twenty-eight; Samuel Peacock, twenty-nine; William Lyon, Jr., and Nathaniel Sanger, thirty-four; Thomas Lyon, thirty-eight; Nathaniel Johnson, thirty-nine; Benjamin Sabin and Samuel Scarborough, forty; Joseph Peake, forty-one; Joseph Bugbee and John Leavens, forty-six; Samuel Craft and Jonathan Peake,[1] forty-nine; Deacon John Chandler, fifty-one; Lieut. Henry Bowen, fifty-three; Edward Morris, fifty-six; and William Lyon Sr., sixty-five.[2]

The first one of the thirty-nine to die was Lieut. Edward Morris, whose gravestone bears the date of 1689, the oldest in the county.[3] The last one of the

---

[1] This Jonathan Peake was the father of Jonathan Peake, Jr., born in 1663, who came to Woodstock in April of 1687.

[2] Lot 43 was given to Clement Corbin soon after the drawing of home lots. The inscription of his rude gravestone reads: "Here lies buried the body of Clement Corbin, aged 70, deceast August ye 1st, 1696."

[3] The inscription on this small gravestone in the burying-ground on Woodstock Hill is read with difficulty and is as follows: "Here lies buried ye body of Lieu. Edward Morris, deceas'd September 14, 1689."

Many of the first settlers now have no stones to mark their graves, and perhaps never had.

thirty-nine to die was Thomas Bacon, who lived to be ninety-six years of age. To show the extreme ages of some of the Woodstock people, it may here be said that Paraclete Skinner, now living, remembers Deacon Jedediah Morse, who died in 1819 at the age of ninety-three, and Deacon Morse was seventeen years old when Col. John Chandler, a first settler, was living; and thirty-two years of age the year that Thomas Bacon, another first settler, died. That is, an inhabitant of this town remembers one who knew some of the first settlers of Woodstock. Lieut. Henry Bowen, one of the first settlers, attained the age of ninety. Deacon Morse's grandmother, who came in April of 1687 to Woodstock with her husband Jonathan Peake, Jr.,[1] likewise lived to be ninety, lacking twelve days. One of the oldest persons that ever lived in Woodstock was Sarah, the daughter of Jonathan Peake, Jr., and the mother of Deacon Morse, who reached the age of ninety-nine, lacking fourty-four days, and who had about her while living three hundred and nineteen descendants.[2] The combined ages of Thomas Bacon, Sarah Morse, and Paraclete Skinner is now two hundred and eighty years. Time alone can tell to what figure their combined ages may attain!

But what a small number in that list of first settlers have descendants bearing the same family name among

---

[1] At that time twenty-four years old.

[2] MSS. of Deacon Jedediah Morse, in the possession of Henry T. Child, of Woodstock.

the citizens of Woodstock to-day! Only James Corbin, William Lyon, John Chandler, Nathaniel Johnson, Benjamin Griggs, Henry Bowen, Joseph Bugbee, Nathaniel Sanger, and John Marcy! But Woodstock is proud to own among the descendants of the first settlers influential and honored citizens of many towns and cities, and some of them, I rejoice to say are here to-day.

The first settlers of Woodstock had the right stuff in them to succeed. After the home-lots were chosen highways were laid out, a grist-mill and saw-mill built, bridges constructed, new inhabitants brought in, and every thing possible was done to make the settlement permanent. A general meeting of the inhabitants was held July 2, 1687, when "John Chandler, Sr., Nathaniel Johnson, Joseph Bugbee, James White, and James Peake, were chosen to order the prudential affairs of the place as selectmen, for the year ensuing."

V.

An effort was now made to get a confirmation of the grant occupied by the new settlers, but as long as Sir Edmund Andros was the Royal Governor of the Province, it was impossible. A delay ensued until William and Mary became sovereigns of Great Britain. The new settlers had not yet an organized town government. The settlement, like the first settlements in Windsor and Hartford, received its name from the mother town.[1] But the New Roxbury people wished to have a name of their own and a town of their own, At the beginning of the year 1690 they chose a committee of three to petition the General Court to substitute a new name for that of New Roxbury. The committee at once conferred with the mother town, for on Jan. 13, 1690, Roxbury held a town meeting at which it was voted to request the General Court to allow the settlement in the Nipmuck country to become a town, to confirm the grant and to give a suitable name. The New Roxbury committee pressed their claims, and on March 18, 1690, the Gen-

[1] Windsor was first called Dorchester and Hartford was first called Newtown.

28

eral Court confirmed the grant and voted that the name of the plantation be Woodstock. We owe the name of Woodstock to Capt. Samuel Sewell[1] who was Chief-Justice of Massachusetts from 1718 to 1728. He has been called "a typical Puritan" and "the Pepys of New England,"—the man who judged the witches of Salem and afterwards repented of it.[2]   In 1690, when Count Frontenac's[3] forces were coming down from Canada upon the settlements of the United Colonies, and Massachusetts determined to ask the help of Connecticut in protecting the upper towns on the Connecticut River, Captain Sewell rode past Woodstock on his way to Connecticut.   He was no doubt on business of state, being one of the Governor's Counsellors, and one of a Committee of Seven of the Council with the same power as the Council to arrange " for setting forth the forces."[4]   The proximity of New Roxbury to Oxford in Massachusetts suggested to him, he tells us, the name of a famous place near old Oxford in England.

[1] Born in England, son of Henry Sewell of Rowley, Mass., and grandson of Henry Sewell, mayor of Coventry, England. In 1684, he became an Assistant.

[2] Memorial " History of Boston," vol. i., 210, 540.

[3] Hildreth's " History of the United States," vol. ii., 130.   Trumbull's " History of Connecticut," vol. i., 401, 402. Palfrey's " Hist. of New England," vol. iv., 46.   Holmes' " Annals of America," vol. i., 430, 431.   Bancroft's " Hist. of the U. S.," vol. iii., 183.

[4] " Collections of the Mass. Hist. Soc.," vol. v., Fifth Series, p. 315, foot-note.   Palfrey's " Hist. of N. E.," vol. iv., 48, foot-note, and appendix.   The other six members of the Committee were Simon Bradstreet (Governor), Sir William Phips (Governor, 1692–95), Maj. Gen. Wait Winthrop, Maj. Elisha Hutchinson, Col. Samuel Shrimpton, and Maj. John Richards.

In his Diary of March 18, 16 $\frac{89}{90}$, Capt. Sewell, says :

" I gave New Roxbury the name of Woodstock, because of its nearness to Oxford, for the sake of Queen Elizabeth, and the notable meetings that have been held at the place bearing that name in England, some of which Dr. Gilbert [1] informed me of when in England. It stands on a Hill. I saw it as I [went] to Coventry, but left it on the left hand. Some told Capt. Ruggles [2] that I gave the name and put words in his mouth to desire of me a Bell for the Town." [3]

Though Judge Sewell, years after his first visit had social relations [4] with some of the inhabitants of Woodstock, there is no evidence to show that he ever gave a bell to the town or to the church. [5] But he gave us something better, a good name,—the name of Wood-

[1] Thomas Gilbert, D.D., of Oxford University, author of "Carmen Congratulatorum." Judge Sewell visited him in England, and was shown by Dr. Gilbert the Bodleian Library, " a very magnificent Thing." See Sewell papers : Fifth Series, Mass. Hist. Soc. Collection, vols. v., vi., vii. We may be allowed to suppose that Dr. Gilbert took Judge Sewell to Woodstock, only eight miles from Oxford University, where the latter perhaps was impressed for the first time with the name and historical associations of Woodstock.

[2] Capt. Ruggles of Roxbury, who died Aug. 15, 1692, of whom Sewell says, in his Diary, Aug. 16th : " Capt. Ruggles also buried this day, died last night, but could not be kept."

[3] Proceedings of Mass. Hist. Soc. for Feb., 1873, p. 399.

[4] Rev. Mr. Dwight, of Woodstock, dined with him Aug. 24, 1718, and made a prayer at his court Nov. 7, 1718. Also see Diary, Jan. 2, 1724 : " Paid Mr. Josiah Dwight of Woodstock in full, of his demands for boarding Madam Usher there about six or seven weeks in the year 1718, £2-11." John Acquittimaug, of Woodstock, an Indian, who lived to be one hundred and fourteen years old, was entertained by Judge Sewell in 1723. *Boston News-Letter*, Aug. 29, 1723. The wills of Woodstock people were proved before " the Honorable Samuel Sewell, Judge of Probate." MSS. of Martin Paine of South Woodstock.

[5] Paraclete Skinner, of Woodstock, who remembers the second meeting-house that was taken down in 1821, says that that structure never had a bell.

stock, associated with the memories of Saxon and Norman Kings, the spot where King Alfred translated "The Consolations of Philosophy," by Boethius, the birth-place of the poet Chaucer, the prison of Queen Elizabeth.[1] History and romance[2] have made illustrious the names of Woodstock and Woodstock Park, and "the notable meetings" spoken of by Judge Sewell as having taken place in Old England have been transferred to the settlement in New England. Surely the name of Woodstock, as applied to the little village of New Roxbury, has proved to be no misnomer.

It should be said that the western part of the town, when it became a settlement years after, revived the old name of New Roxbury. The church in West Woodstock belonged to what was called the Parish of New Roxbury, or the Second Precinct of Woodstock.[3]

---

[1] While in custody at Woodstock, Queen Elizabeth, according to the chronicler, Raphael Holinshed, wrote with a diamond on a pane of glass in her room these words :

> " Much suspected—of me
> Nothing proved can be,
> Quoth Elizabeth, prisoner."

[2] Sir Walter Scott's novel of " Woodstock."

[3] The last time that the name of New Roxbury, as applied to the name of the whole town, appears in the Proprietors' Records of Woodstock is March 18, 1689. The first time the name of Woodstock appears is May 26, 1690 : Woodstock Records.

VI.

The most pressing duty for our ancestors to perform, after securing a name and legalized status for the town, was the settlement of "an able, orthodox, godly minister." The Rev. Josiah Dwight, a graduate of Harvard College in the class of 1687, received the appointment, and was installed October 17, 1690, receiving £40 the first year, £50 the second, and £60 the third year and thereafter. It was with difficulty, however, that these sums were paid, and when, some years after, the account was settled by the payment of what was due, he gave a receipt in full "from the beginning of the world to May 6, 1696." A home lot was allowed Mr. Dwight according to the original drawing of lots, and arrangements were made to build a home for him immediately after his settlement. The following year,[1] it was determined to construct a house of worship, which was completed early[2] in 1694. This was the first meeting-house in Windham County, and here gathered, on Sabbath days, the settlers from miles around. The people of Pomfret attended church in this rude structure until 1715, when their own society was organized.

[1] 1691.   [2] March.

The officers of the new town elected in 1690 [1] were John Chandler, Sr., William Bartholomew, Benjamin Sabin, John Leavens, and Joseph Bugbee, as selectmen, and John Chandler, Jr., as town clerk. All of those men to-day have descendants in Woodstock or its immediate vicinity. At that time, the men of Woodstock imposed a fine of one and six pence upon every one who failed to attend the town meeting, and six pence an hour for tardiness. Disputes regarding titles to land, and the boundary line dividing the north half of the town, and disputes with the mother-town regarding this northern half, which belonged to Roxbury according to the terms of the grant, were vexatious, and not in every respect creditable to Woodstock. But Roxbury's interest in the northern half of Woodstock continued till 1757, when the lands had all been sold or become individual property. Large tracts, however, were held by Roxbury and Woodstock speculators for many years afterward.

Troubles with the Indians, who returned to their old hunting and fishing haunts after the settlement of the town, broke out in 1696,[2] and again in 1700 and 1704, and even as late as 1724. When a war broke out abroad, there was trouble with the Indians at home. When an Indian outbreak was threatened, the town

[1] Town meeting November 27th and 28th.

[2] Woodstock, at this time, was under the restrictions of frontier towns. It was called a "frontier town" in 1695.—Mass. Hist. Society Proceedings, 1871–1873, p. 395.

received some military assistance from the colony government. Such threatened outbreaks retarded the progress of the settlement.

After discussing the question for several years, the town determined, in 1719,[1] to erect a new meeting-house near the burying-ground, instead of at the south end of the village, where the old building stood, yet so straitened were the people in their circumstances that they applied to the General Court in Boston, requesting that the unoccupied lands of the residents and non-residents of the town be taxed to the extent of £250, to be applied to the building of a church. As the non-residents' lands were almost entirely in the north half of the grant, and belonged to Roxbury people, Roxbury stoutly opposed the tax in a memorial to the General Court. When the General Court refused the petition, Woodstock asked to be excused from sending her representative to Boston. The town's representative at this time, in fact the first and only representative for many years, was Captain John Chandler, who, like his father Deacon John Chandler, was one of the first settlers. He surveyed lands in Woodstock and neighboring towns, and owned large tracts of territory in Connnecticut and Massachusetts. To avoid the necessity of sending to Boston to have deeds recorded and wills proven, Captain Chandler tried to get the consent of the General Court in

[1] December 28th.

1720 for the formation of a new county, to be called Worcester County, of which Woodstock should be a part, but a delay ensued until 1731, when Captain, now Colonel, Chandler was successful. Woodstock became one of the most prominent towns of Worcester County, and John Chandler was made Chief Justice of the Court of Common Pleas and General Sessions.[1]

[1] Lincoln's "History of Worcester County."

VII.

Ecclesiastical affairs have been so interwoven with town affairs, that it is impossible to give a sketch of Woodstock without giving a history of the churches. It may, however, be done briefly, as others have been appointed to speak specially for the different church organizations of the town. Though the first minister, the Rev. Josiah Dwight, was of the " Standing Order," so-called, and believed in the Cambridge platform, yet he was suspected of theological looseness and, besides many idiosyncrasies, was accused of "speculating in the wild lands of Killingly." The first settlers had no end of trouble with him, especially regarding money matters, and he was finally removed September 3, 1726. The next regular minister was Rev. Amos Throop, who was installed May 24, 1727. Like Mr. Dwight, he was a graduate of Harvard College, and came to Woodstock at the age of twenty-five. Naturally he found fault when the town attempted to pay him his salary in the depreciated currency of the time. But the eight years of his ministry endeared him to the settlement, and his sudden death in 1735 [1] was keenly felt by his

[1] Sept. 7th.

parishioners. The town assumed the expense of his gravestone, upon which may be read these words :

> " O cruel death, to snatch from us below,
> One fit to live within the spheres on high ;
> But since the great Creator orders so,
> Here at his feet he doth submissive lie."

During the pastorate of Mr. Throop the western part of the town[1] had received some settlers, mostly the sons of Woodstock's first settlers. In 1727 Joshua Chandler took possession of some land that had been given him by his father, Col. John Chandler, and representatives of the families of Child, Corbin, Lyon, Aspinwall, Bugbee, Morris, Marcy, Morse, Payson, Perrin, Johnson, Frizzel, Griggs, and Paine soon followed. In 1733[2] the town arranged to have a school-house built in this part of the town, and, the settlers increasing, West Parish desired[3] to have religious services of its own for four months of the year at the expense of the whole town. This request, it was argued, was only fair, inasmuch as the western half was obliged to contribute to the support of the Church on the Hill. But the town refused[4] to assume any of the charges. After trying the experiment for two winters, the West Parish people found the expense of supporting both ministers to be

---

[1] Manuscript Records of Second Precinct of Woodstock, or Parish of New Roxbury, in the possession of G. Clinton Williams, of West Woodstock.

[2] May 16th.

[3] Petition to town Nov. 2, 1736.

[4] July, 1737.

too great a burden, and they therefore again asked [1] the help of the town, and were refused. They still persisted, and petitioned [2] that the western half might be formed into a distinct township. Town meetings were held, and at last permission was given [3] them to address the General Court in Boston on the subject. But their petition to the General Court was dismissed. The West Woodstock people, however, insisted on the formation of a parish where they could worship God in their own fashion, and not be obliged to aid any church outside of their parish. They were willing to give up all idea of a town of their own. This modified request was now made to the town [4] and to the General Court.[5] The General Court complied by passing an act in 1743,[6] incorporating the district as "The West Parish of Woodstock." A meeting was at once held,[7] at which it was determined to survey the line dividing the two portions of the town. West Parish was now called by the old name of New Roxbury. These acts were afterwards approved by the General Assembly of Connecticut when Woodstock withdrew from under the jurisdiction of Massachusetts.[8] In 1747 Rev. Stephen Williams was ordained pastor.

The church [9] on the Hill was under the pastorate of

[1] 1739. [2] Oct. 2, 1741. [3] April, 1742.
[4] Letter of Aug., 1742, to selectmen.
[5] Nov. 18, 1742. [6] Sept. 14th. [7] In the school-house Sept. 27th.
[8] Line dividing East and West Parishes approved by General Assembly of Connecticut in 1753, and name of New Roxbury approved in 1754.
[9] The old First Church. See Records of First and Third Congregational Churches, and Miss Larned's " History of Windham County."

Rev. Abel S. Stiles, who had been ordained in 1737.[1] But the fact that Mr. Stiles was a graduate of Yale College[2] instead of Harvard, as his two predecessors had been, and his family connections[3] were all with Connecticut, his parishioners were led to believe that he would favor the " Saybrook Platform " of faith, rather than the " Cambridge Platform," and if there was one thing our ancestors abhorred quite as much as Episcopacy or popery it was the " Saybrook Platform." To be tainted with that form of faith, as was the case with Mr. Stiles after his settlement in Woodstock, was heresy indeed, and Woodstock was determined, according to her grant of 1683, to have none other but an " able, orthodox, godly minister." Instead of attending the Association of Ministers in Massachusetts, Mr. Stiles preferred the meetings of the Windham County Association in Connecticut, and when Woodstock became a part of Connecticut the troubles with Mr. Stiles increased. Councils were held. Pastor and parishioners tried to discipline each other. The General Assembly of Connecticut was appealed to. Threats—even violence was resorted to. But without going into the details of this long-protracted struggle, let it be said that there were two

[1] July 27th.   [2] Class of 1733.

[3] He was the son of John Stiles, who belonged to one of the oldest families of Windsor, and was the brother of Rev. Isaac Stiles, a graduate of Yale College in the class of 1722, and was uncle of Ezra Stiles, President of Yale College. President Stiles often visited Woodstock after his uncle had settled at Muddy Brook, now called East Woodstock.

parties in the controversy, one side sympathizing with Mr. Stiles in his ~~more-liberal~~ theological views, and the other side at first insisting on a minister who should conform in all respects to the " Standing Order," and afterwards opposed to Mr. Stiles personally as well as theologically. The Stiles party had favored, while the anti-Stiles party had opposed, the annexation of Woodstock to Connecticut. The result of the quarrel was a break in the church in 1760. The North Society was constituted by act[1] of the General Assembly, and Mr. Stiles and his followers went to Muddy Brook. Thus was formed the Third Congregational Church of Woodstock, and here Mr. Stiles continued to preach until his death in 1783.[2] When it was determined in 1831, by the church in East Woodstock, to build a new meeting-house on the spot of the old one erected in 1767, the people in Village Corners objected to the location and formed a society of their own —the Fourth Congregational Church of Woodstock.

After the departure of Mr. Stiles the First Church was without a pastor for three years. Much time was spent in " going after ministers." The young Yale graduates who preached on trial did not please the church, whose sympathies were still with Massachusetts. Finally the Rev. Abiel Leonard, a graduate of Harvard College,[3] was installed on June 23, 1763. Of the twelve churches asked to assist in the ordination only

[1] Oct., 1761.   [2] July 25th, at the age of 74.   [3] Class of 1759.

one[1] was a Connecticut organization. In fact it was
not until the year 1815 that the church, after an adherence to the Cambridge order of faith for a hundred
and twenty-five years, finally accepted the " Saybrook
Platform," and joined the Connecticut association.
The church was prosperous under Mr. Leonard.
Largely owing to his influence the quarrel between
the First and Third Churches was healed.[2] In 1775,
on the breaking out of the Revolutionary War, Mr.
Leonard was made Chaplain of the Third Regiment
of Connecticut troops. The church, at the request of
the commander, Colonel, afterwards General, Israel
Putnam, granted the necessary leave of absence.
The following year Washington and Putnam joined in
writing a letter[3] to the church at Woodstock asking for
a continued leaved of absence for Mr. Leonard, prais-
ing him in the highest terms, and saying :

" He is employed in the glorious work of attending
to the morals of a brave people who are fighting for
their liberties—the liberties of the people of Woodstock—the liberties of all America."

Agreeable a gentleman as Mr. Leonard was, he was
suddenly superseded while on a visit to Woodstock,
and on receiving the mortifying news when *en route*
to join the army he at once committed suicide.

[1] Killingly.
[2] Vote of First Church passed Dec. 8, 1766.
[3] Letter dated Cambridge, March 24, 1776.

If ever there was an " able, orthodox, godly minister," of the true Massachusetts type, such as old Woodstock always loved to have, he was the Rev. Eliphalet
Lyman, who was ordained in 1779. Although a
graduate of Yale College,[1] he fulfilled the conditions of
the Cambridge Platform, and continued pastor of the
First Church for forty-five years, and was warmly interested in the religious and educational development
of the town. He was the last of the historic ministers
of Woodstock. He was respected and he was feared.
The boys stopped playing ball when " Old Priest
Lyman," in cocked hat and knee breeches, remembered
by some of you here to-day, walked up the common.

[1] Class of 1776.

VIII.

It should now be related how Woodstock, settled under Massachusetts, became a part of the State of Connecticut. Massachusetts claimed Woodstock, because the grant was supposed to lie within her chartered bounds as surveyed in 1642, and that claim was what Major Daniel Gookin referred to when he rebuked the agent of Uncas in 1674, during his visit with John Eliot, at Woodstock. But Massachusetts did not believe that the line of 1642 was wrong when she confirmed the grant to the Roxbury settlers. She even censured Woodstock for daring to ask Connecticut to confirm a portion of the grant that fell south of this line. Though Connecticut justly held she was entitled to Woodstock, according to the terms of her charter, she was, nevertheless, willing to forego her claim to this town, provided Massachusetts would allow her to have the jurisdiction over other territory claimed by both colonies. But the repeated attempts to settle the controversy failed, and it was not till 1713 that an agreement was finally concluded. For the privilege of having jurisdiction over Woodstock and the other towns claimed by both sides, Massachusetts agreed to compensate Connecticut, by giving her unimproved lands in Western Massachusetts and New Hampshire. These lands were therefore called " equivalent lands," and were sold by Connecticut for $2,274, and the money given to Yale College. Woodstock was entirely satisfied with this agreement, as all her associations were with Massachusetts. But in 1747 the town thought that her taxes, which had been increased owing to the French and Spanish wars,[1] would be lighter, and her privileges greater, if she followed Suffield, Enfield, and Somers " in trying to get off to Connecticut." So Woodstock applied to Connecticut, claiming that the agreement of 1713 had been made without her consent. After much deliberation, Connecticut voted in 1749 to receive the town, and declared the agreement of 1713 not binding. Woodstock was delighted at being received into Connecticut, and at a memorable town meeting[2] made Thomas Chandler and Henry Bowen the first members of the General Assembly. Though Woodstock has since 1749 been a part of this State, Massachusetts would never formally yield jurisdiction over the town, and even as late as 1768 warned the inhabitants not to pay taxes to Connecticut. In fact had it not been for the Revolution, Massachusetts might still be claiming Wood-

---

[1] Hutchinson's " History of Massachusetts," vol. iii., 6–8 ; vol. ii., 363–396.
[2] July 28, 1749.

stock.[1]   It might be added that Woodstock, in being annexed to Connecticut, lost about three thousand acres north of the colony line.   This strip of land was known as the " Middlesex Gore " for forty-five years, and was annexed to Dudley and Sturbridge in 1794.

After becoming a part of Connecticut, Woodstock was anxious that the northern half of Windham County should be made into a separate county, of which Woodstock should be the shire-town, but as Pomfret also desired the county seat, and as the State seemed unwilling to act, the project fell through.[2]

[1] Woodstock speaks of Massachusetts' repeated claims in a memorial to Conn. Gen. Assembly, May 2, 1771.

[2] Gen. Putnam was much interested in this project.   A meeting to promote the idea was held at his house in Pomfret, Feb. 11, 1771.   The State again refused the application for a new county, when Pomfret applied in 1786 for a new county, "with Pomfret for shire-town."

IX.

Woodstock's military glory is something of which she may well be proud. Representatives of the Morris, Bowen, Hubbard, and Johnson families, who came to Woodstock in 1686, fought under Captain Isaac Johnson, of Roxbury, in King Philip's War, and were in the famous Narragansett battle in 1675, when Captain Johnson was killed.[1] For the first forty years after the settlement of the town the Indian troubles made every man acquainted with the use of fire-arms, and when in later years there appeared no danger at home, our ancestors were ready to fight abroad either savage or foreign foes. In 1724, Colonel John Chandler received orders from Boston to impress twenty Woodstock men for the frontier service,[2] which meant that they should fight Indians in Central Massachusetts. When the news of the war between France and Great Britain was received in Boston in 1744,[3] fifty[4] men

[1] Captain Johnson was the father of Nathaniel Johnson, and father-in-law of Lieutenant Henry Bowen, both first settlers of Woodstock.

[2] " The Chandler Family," by Dr. George Chandler.

[3] England declared war against France March 31st.

[4] Seven hundred men from Massachusetts, of which Woodstock was then a part, were impressed for this service.

from Colonel Thomas Chandler's[1] regiment guarded the frontier, and history declares that this regiment, commanded by a Woodstock man, rendered efficient service in the capture of Louisburg in 1745.[2] In 1748, before the treaty of Aix la Chapelle had been signed,[3] the death was chronicled of several Woodstock men who had gone up into New Hampshire to fight[4] the Indians with a company of colony troops. In the French and Indian War[5] for the conquest of Canada, the families of Bacon, Bugbee, Child, Corbin, Chandler, Frizzel, Griggs, Holmes, Lyon, Marcy, McClellan, Manning, Peake, and Perrin had representatives who distinguished themselves in the service. Woodstock and Pomfret boys composed the company of Captain Israel Putnam in this war. The McClellan and Lyon of the Seven Years' War were the McClellan and Lyon of the Revolution, and were of the same family as the McClellan and Lyon so celebrated and so much beloved in our own Civil War.

The service rendered by Woodstock during the Revolution was most valuable. The town voted to purchase as few British goods as possible, and

[1] Lieut.-Col. Thomas Chandler was the son of Col. John Chandler, and was Woodstock's first representative to the General Assembly of Connecticut. Ante p. 44.

[2] The forces were furnished by New Hampshire, Massachusetts, and Connecticut, and amounted to 4,070. [3] October 7th.

[4] Fight at "Charlestown, No. 4," New Hampshire, May 2, 1748, in which Peter Perrin and Aaron Lyon, of Woodstock, were killed.

[5] Or the Seven Years' War (1753–1760).

sent sixty-five fat sheep to Boston as a contribution to
alleviate what the town records call "the distressed
and suffering circumstances" of that city. Captain
Elisha Child, Charles Church Chandler, Jedediah
Morse, Captain Samuel McClellan, and Nathaniel
Child, were appointed a committee ' "for maintaining
a correspondence with the towns of this and the neighboring colonies." The spirit of revolution, which had
been growing, rose to fever-heat when the powder
stored in Cambridge by the patriots was removed, in
September of 1774, to Boston. The news flew as fast
through the New England towns as horses' hoofs could
take it. A son of Esquire Wolcott brought the news
to Curtis' tavern in Dudley, and a son of Captain Clark
carried it to his father's house in Woodstock, where it
was carried to Colonel Israel Putnam in Pomfret.[2]
The young men of Woodstock did not wait for the call
to arms. They hurried to Cambridge, and, with the
inhabitants of that and other towns, were with difficulty restrained from marching into Boston to demand,
with their loaded muskets, the return of the powder.
At the very beginning of the Revolution Woodstock
was eager to do its duty. When the cry went through
New England that blood had been shed at that " birth-
place of American liberty," the historic Lexington, one
hundred and eighty-nine men from Woodstock

---

[1] At town meeting, June 21, 1774.
[2] Miss Ellen D. Larned's " History of Windham County."

answered that call.[1]   Ephraim Manning, Stephen
Lyon, Asa Morris, and William Frizzel were officers in
Colonel Israel Putnam's regiment when that regiment
was stationed at Cambridge, while Captain Samuel
McClellan had charge of the troop of horse, of which
John Flynn was trumpeter.   Captain Nathaniel Marcy,
Captains Elisha and Benjamin Child, Lieut. Josiah
Child, Captain Daniel Lyon, Jabez and John Fox,
Samuel Perry, and many other Woodstock men, ren-
dered services in this war equally efficient.   When
Samuel Perry, in his old age, used to go up to the
store on Woodstock Hill in the evening, the boys
would ask him to tell them about the battle of Bunker
Hill, and would always ask if he had killed any of the
British in that battle.   " I don't know whether I killed
any," was his reply, " but I took good aim, fired, and
saw them drop!"   Another Woodstock name, always
honored at home as another of the same family name is
to-day no less honored abroad, was Dr. David Holmes
He had served as surgeon in the French war, and—

——" lived to see
The bloodier strife that made our nation free,
To serve with willing toil, with skilful hand,
The war-worn saviors of the bleeding land." [2]

[1] There is no evidence to prove the reiterated statement that one hundred
and eighty-nine Woodstock men fought at the battle of Bunker Hill.   This
number was stationed at Cambridge, and some of them may have been at
Bunker Hill.

[2] Oliver Wendell Holmes at Roseland Park, July 4, 1877.

When Washington assumed charge of the troops in Cambridge, the Rev. Abiel Leonard, the beloved pastor of the First Church at Woodstock, preached most acceptably. Washington heard him and became his warm friend. Woodstock's importance during the Revolution was considerable. One line of stages between Woodstock and New London and another line between Woodstock and New Haven and Hartford were established, which carried the war news weekly to be distributed through the colony and thence taken to New York. During the entire war Woodstock did more than her share. While there were many from this town who served the patriot cause with glory to themselves and honor to Woodstock, the name of Capt., afterwards Gen., Samuel McClellan stands out the most illustrious. When the currency of the Continentals had depreciated and no funds were forthcoming with which to pay the soldiers, Gen., or more exactly Col., McClellan advanced £1,000 from his own private purse to pay the men of his regiment. But a memorial of the Revolution in which Woodstock may well take the greatest pride is found in the historic elm-trees in South Woodstock, planted by the wife of General McClellan on receiving the news of the battle of Lexington. All honor to the men of Woodstock who fought for and gained their liberties in the Revolution, and all honor to their wives, who were equally patriotic at home!

In the War of 1812 Woodstock was also ready to do its duty. When Major William Flynn, of Woodstock Hill, received the news, one evening just after dark, that several British men-of-war were hovering about New London, and that it was in danger of attack, he rode horseback about the country during the night, to see officers and men and warn them to assemble on the Common at noon the next day ; but when he returned to his home at sunrise he found the Common covered with soldiers ready to go to New London immediately. The patriotic spirit always characteristic of Woodstock was conspicuous in the War of 1812.

Woodstock was no less patriotic during the Rebellion. When President Lincoln called for volunteers to maintain the unity of the country, this town did her full share in that struggle. Many of you remember attending the funeral of General Nathaniel Lyon, who was killed at the beginning of the war and was buried with military honors in our neighboring town of Eastford. Though not a native of Woodstock, Gen. Lyon was descended from an honored family which has been conspicuous in the history of this town from the day of its settlement. But a name even more illustrious is that of Gen. George B. McClellan, whose grandfather was a native of Woodstock, and whose great-grandfather was Gen. Samuel McClellan, and who himself, as a boy, visited the town. You saw him beneath these very trees two years ago. You heard him speak

at that time words of love for Woodstock and words
of welcome to distinguished strangers. His voice is
no longer heard, but the name of General McClellan
will be remembered as long as the name of Woodstock
itself shall last. Blessed then be the memory of Gen.
George B. McClellan! Woodstock will ever cherish
his services and the services of all its sons who fought
for their country in the terrible struggle between the
North and the South! The graves in the different
burying-grounds of the town, that you annually decor-
ate with flowers, tell more eloquently than words what
Woodstock did during the Civil War.

X.

Woodstock has never been negligent in the cause of education. As soon as the settlement became an organized town, John Chandler, Jr., was appointed to instruct the children to write and cipher. As the town grew in population, it was divided into school districts. In 1739 was established the United English Library for the Propagation of Christianity and Useful Knowledge. Col. John Chandler was the moderator at the first meeting, and the Rev. Abel Stiles, John May, Benjamin Child, and Penfel Bowen, of Woodstock, and leading citizens of Pomfret and Killingly, assisted in the organization.[1] It was Gen. Samuel McClellan and his sons John and James McClellan, the Rev. Eliphalet Lyman, William Bowen, Parker Comings, Nehemiah Child, Ebenezer Smith, William Potter, Hezekiah Bugbee, Benjamin Lyon, Ebenezer Skinner, and Amos Paine who established Woodstock Academy, at the beginning of the present century, and the influence of that honored institution has been deep and far-reach-

[1] Rev. Abel Styles subscribed the largest sum, £30. He was fond of *belles-lettres*, and in a communication to his church, speaks of "his beloved studies." Under his inspiration and instruction, Woodstock and Pomfret young men entered Yale College.

ing. But who can measure the good done by Woodstock Academy, or by the different churches and other
organizations of the town? Such institutions are our
heritage, and our duty and privilege it is to improve
their character and transmit them to future generations,
with the memories and traditions of the town itself.

XI.

Citizens of Woodstock, listen while I call the roll of some of the distinguished men who have lived or were born in the town. Of the first settlers was Col. John Chandler, probably the most distinguished citizen that Woodstock had during its first century, the man who made Woodstock known and respected throughout New England. His descendants include the Rev. Thomas Bradbury Chandler, D.D., Winthrop Chandler, the artist, the Hon. John Church Chandler, Judge John Winthrop Chandler, and others, who have been prominent in Woodstock and throughout the country. No one of the first settlers was more distinguished than Edward Morris, who died three years after the town was settled. His family was prominent in the history of old Roxbury, and all through the last century in Woodstock. Commodore Charles Morris, a native [1] of Woodstock and well known in the War of 1812, and his son, Commodore George N. Morris, Commander in the Civil War of the United States sloop-of-war *Cumberland* in Hampton Roads, belong to the

[1] 1784-1856.

same family, as well as the Hon. J. F. Morris, of
Hartford, whom I am sure we are glad to welcome as our presiding officer to-day. John Marcy,
a first settler, was the ancestor of Hon. William

Learned ~~Leonard~~ Marcy, Governor of the State of New York,
Secretary of War under President Polk and Secretary
of State under President Pierce. Abiel Holmes,[1]
D.D., LL.D., author of "Annals of America," and his
father, Dr. David Holmes, a surgeon in the French and
Revolutionary wars, were born in Woodstock, and
were descended from John Holmes, a first settler.
Abiel Holmes' son, Oliver Wendell Holmes, though
not born in Woodstock, will be remembered, I am
sure, for the beautiful tribute he paid his ancestors in
the poem he read in this very park in 1877. The
name of Morse has always been identified with Woodstock. Deacon Jedediah Morse held about all the
offices in town that he could lawfully hold, and was
deacon of the First Church for forty-three years.
His son, the Rev. Jedediah Morse, D.D., a graduate of
Yale College and the father of American geography,
was also born in Woodstock. His grandson was Prof.
Samuel F. B. Morse, who was more widely known as
the inventor of the electric telegraph. Another Woodstock boy was General William Eaton [2] who ran away,
from home at the age of sixteen to enter the Revolutionary War, and was distinguished during the first

[1] 1763-1837.   [2] 1764-1804.

years of the century as the protector of American commerce in the Mediterranean. Amasa Walker, too, was born in Woodstock, the father of political economy in this country, or better still, the father of Gen. Francis A. Walker, the respected President of the School of Technology in Boston. Another honored name in Woodstock is that of Williams, including Samuel Williams, Sr., the Commissioner of Roxbury in the settlement of New Roxbury, the Rev. Stephen Williams, the first pastor of the church at West Parish, and Jared W. Williams, the Governor of Vermont and a native of this town. Governors, members of Congress, men distinguished in law, theology, and medicine, in trade and on the farm, have been born in Woodstock. The roll of honor could be multiplied ; but in speaking of the distinguished men it would be impossible to forget the lessons taught, the struggle, endured, and the sacrifices made by the mothers of Woodstock, who all through these two centuries have inspired their sons with feelings that have made them industrious, honored, and religious. Praise be, therefore, to the women of Woodstock ! This town has the right to be proud of such noble sons and daughters, and we have the right to be proud that such a town as old Woodstock has nourished us and blessed us with such memories and influences.

XII.

What has the town done to make us proud of
it ? It has exerted an influence for good upon the
country wherever its inhabitants have settled. Such
settlements have been many. During the early
history of the plantation, Woodstock men assisted
largely in the settlement of Ashford, Pomfret, Killingly, and other neighboring towns. As the surplus
population increased, migrations were made to the
wild regions of Vermont and New Hampshire. Later
came the settlements made by Connecticut, in the
provinces of New York and Pennsylvania, in which
Woodstock families were almost without exception
represented. At the close of the Revolution the wave
of emigration extended still farther West, and some
of the oldest families in Ohio trace their ancestry back
to this very town. To-day Woodstock has its representatives in almost every State in the Union, and the
material growth and prosperity of the country has been
in full measure owing to the settlements made by men
from towns in New England like Woodstock. The
ideas inherited from Puritan ancestors and modified
according to existing circumstances have made towns,

58

cities, even States, in which the whole country to-day takes the warmest pride. The man who inherits New England traditions from towns like Woodstock is worth more to the country than an army of Anarchists and Socialists.

Woodstock is distinguished, too, for its " notable meetings," inherited from the Woodstock in England, of which Judge Sewell speaks. The first " notable meeting " was when John Eliot preached to the Indians on Plaine Hill. The second " notable meeting " was when the first settlers drew their home lots in Wabba-quasset Hall. The third " notable meeting " was at the funeral of Col. John Chandler in 1743, attended by the leading men in the colonies of Massachusetts and Connecticut. The church meetings of the last century, the town meeting when Woodstock transferred its allegiance to Connecticut, meetings during the Revolution, the old " training days " on Woodstock Common, have been followed by no end of " notable meetings " during the present century. But the one " notable meeting " that those of us present here to-day have in mind, was when Ulysses S. Grant, General of the Army, Savior of the Country and President of the United States, visited the town in 1870.

But the chief glory of the town of Woodstock has been its love of local law. The source of the power of the continental nations of Europe may be traced back through the centuries to the village communities and Teutonic townships. In the mark, tithing, and parish of England the same principle of local self-government may be seen ; and so our own nation's greatness, through Anglo-Saxon inheritance, has its source, not in the State, city, or county, but in the little school districts, villages, and towns of New England. Woodstock has been like a miniature republic, and has always believed in the supremacy of local law. Its refusal to send its representative to the General Court at Boston unless it could tax its own property as it pleased, and the refusal, for political reasons, of its delegates at the State Convention in 1788 to vote for the ratification of the Constitution of the United States, are instances of the extreme independence of Woodstock. What it conscientiously believed, the town has never been slow to proclaim. Tenacious as Woodstock has always been of its privileges and its rights, its loyalty to the country, from the day the thirteen colonies became a nation, has never been questioned.

XIII.

I have given scarce more than a sketch in outline of what the history of Woodstock has been during the two hundred years since that historic band of brave boys and sturdy men, of deft-handed girls and sober matrons, swarmed like bees from the Roxbury hive[1] and settled on the Wabbaquasset hills. What Woodstock's history shall be remains for you, men and women of Woodstock, to develop. The fathers have kept bright the honest traditions and stout independence, the industrious thrift and religious faith which their Puritan fathers brought to the new settlement. The sons of this generation can be trusted to preserve and transmit them to their descendants. You, men of Woodstock, have your duties in the family, on the farm, toward your schools, and to your churches. All that the fathers have done puts an added obligation upon you. The improvement and development of the town depend on the individual exertions of its citizens. If you are young, infuse some of your own enthusiasm and intelligence into its different organizations. If you

[1] Cotton Mather: " Massachusetts soon became like a hive overstocked with bees, and many thought of swarming into new plantations."

are old, remember these institutions in a substantial way. Woodstock will be what you make it. Michel Angelo saw in the block the exquisite unsculptured statue. Many blows of the chisel were necessary to disclose the perfect ideal to the eyes of a wondering world. In thought, in plan, in ideal, this town has been almost a perfect organization ; but only those whose high vision is willing to pierce through all encrusting imperfections shall be the artists whose toil and sacrifices shall make this dear, noble, historic town of Woodstock an honor to the State and a blessing to its citizens. It is said that old John Eliot, from the high pulpit in Roxbury, used to pray every Sabbath for the new settlers at Woodstock. The words of those prayers are not preserved, but may the spirit of them come down through the centuries to inspire the hearts of all who inherit the blood of the early settlers of this ancient town. God, our fathers' God, bless old Woodstock !

INDEX.

63